Al B[signature]

Heyward the Horse and

The Founding of Charleston

Written & Illustrated by Andrew Barton

JACE, EMARIE & BROOKS,
See you in Charleston!

Copyright © 2021 by Andrew Barton

All rights reserved. This book or any portion thereof
may not be reproduced or used in any manner whatsoever
without the express written permission of the publisher
except for the use of brief quotations in a book review.

Typeset in Hoefler Text and Gill Sans

First Printing, 2021
Printed in South Korea

ISBN 978-0-9997817-2-2

www.HeywardtheHorse.com

For my daughter, Georgia.

Good morning, my dear. Let's go out and see.
the peoples and steeples of Charleston, SC.

I'm Heyward the Horse, city guide number one.

I'm proud of my job and I make learning fun!

I love my dear city, both pretty and grand.
But how did it come to be built where we stand?

That's a fun story. It starts with a horse.

My great great great great great great great grandpa, of course.

He set out from England a long time ago
and founded the city we've all come to know.

But history is hard to imagine for me.
Perhaps there's a way we can go back and see!

Remember my secret? My special bow tie.
When I put it on, we can magically fly!

So pile in the carriage. We're zooming with speed.

Straight to the 17th century indeed!

But what does that mean? The question is fair.
To build a new city for profit and share[2]!

So through thunder and lightning, and rain at its worst,
sailed my brave ancestor, Heyward the First.

A hero, a captain, a leader, a dad.
A mighty wise stallion – impeccably clad!

They sailed up a harbor, a river, a creek.
The Captain jumped up, and he started to speak.

"Unload those barrels. Cut down those trees. Let's build some shelters before we all freeze."

Charles Towne, they named it (to honor the King). It grew bigger and bigger and filled with offspring.

They traded with locals[3]. They farmed off the land. They built a wood wall, and they built it by hand.

But after ten years, Captain stood to declare,
"Pack up our village. Let's move over there!"

They started all over to live by the sea,
the new name was Charlestown[4] (one word and one "e").

This time the wall wasn't made of big sticks.
They built it from scratch out of tabby and bricks[5].

Heyward spoke up, "Let's protect what we own, so Pirates and Spaniards will leave us alone."

Many ships floated in from the sea far and wide.
They loaded up goods[6] and sailed out with the tide.

There's much more to tell, but our time is so short.
To sum it all up, we became a rich port.

Our journey ends soon; say goodbye to the past.

We're flying back home and we're coming in fast!

I'm glad to be back and I hope that you find learning our history has opened your mind.

That's all for today, but whenever you're near, come back to see Heyward in Charleston, my dear.

A TRUE HISTORY

In April 1670, a ship named Carolina sailed up the Ashley River and settled on a marshy point on the river's western bank. The small group of English settlers was skeptical of their new home. Having originally intended to settle further south toward Port Royal, they chose instead to follow the advice of Kiawah natives and moved their settlement northward to an area they christened Albemarle Point. It was a wise choice. Here, they realized, the new colony would be not only further away from enemy-occupied Spanish Florida, but also certainly more easily defensible from French invaders, or worse, pirates. By November, having established a reasonably fortified foothold in the vast Carolina Lowcountry, the settlement was renamed "Charles Towne" after England's reigning monarch, King Charles II.

As more and more settlers arrived, governing officials were eager to expand. In 1672, they looked eastward across the Ashley River to a high-grounded peninsula. The area was named Oyster Point because of the literal tons of oyster shells piled on its riverbanks. Plans were soon in place to resettle the entire community there.

A grid of streets was mapped out and, by 1680, Charles Town had relocated and soon after became a bustling city of over 1,000 people.

To strengthen the town's defenses, workers in the 1690s constructed a wall along the waterfront. It was built with a locally made mortar called "tabby." In 1703, with the outbreak of Queen Anne's War between England and Spain, the city was quick to expand its wall around the rest of the city. They even built a drawbridge to serve as a formal landward entrance into town. Once complete, Charlestown (now being written as one word and without the "e") was the only English walled city in North America.

Charlestown became a vibrant city as the years went on. The wall was long gone by the 1750s as trade and commerce flourished. Eventually, years of tension with England lead to war and, ultimately, American independence. Once the long Revolution was all over in 1783, Charlestown incorporated as a city and its name was altered to that which we still use today: Charleston.

HOOFNOTES

[1] Eight of his chums (page 10)

In 1663, King Charles II granted the Carolina colony to eight Lords Proprietors, who had near total control of the territory, including establishing government and commerce. For the new Carolina settlers, however, the proprietors' support was inadequate. In 1729, after years of bickering, the Lords Proprietors yielded ownership to the crown, and South Carolina became a royal colony.

[2] Profit & share (page 11)

Once Charlestown was established as a primary port city, its agriculture and inter-colonial trade grew. To handle the workload, merchants imported and sold thousands of enslaved Africans as well as Native American slaves to plant and harvest crops, such as indigo and rice. By the 1720s, merchants and planters were making immense amounts of money.

[3] Traded with locals (page 17)

When English settlers arrived in their new home, they met several tribes of Native Americans. The settlers traded with the Native Americans and learned about coastal living from these native people.

[4] Charlestown (page 19)

Named after King Charles II, there's still debate over Charleston's original spelling. "Charles Towne" (with an "e") appears in 17th-century documents. Not much later, however, "Charles Town" (without the "e") and "Charlestown" (one word) both appear regularly during most of the 18th century. The city was formally chartered in 1783, and its name shortened to the one we still use today: "Charleston."

[5] Tabby and bricks (page 20)

Bricks were the choice material for Lowcountry homes, military fortifications, and other urban buildings. To hold the bricks together, English settlers used a mixture known as "tabby" created by combining water, sand, ash, and crushed and broken oyster shells.

[6] Loaded up goods (page 22)

For the South Carolina colony to be successful, it had to provide useful products that could be shipped back to England and then sold. Early on these materials included timber and naval stores such as pitch and tar. Deerskins, obtained through trade with Native Americans, were among the most vital exports to fuel England's demand for quality leather.

About the Author and Illustrator

Andrew Barton is a designer, illustrator and children's book author in Charleston, S.C. He lives in West Ashley with his wife and three children. He enjoys drawing, reading, writing, boardgames and the outdoors.

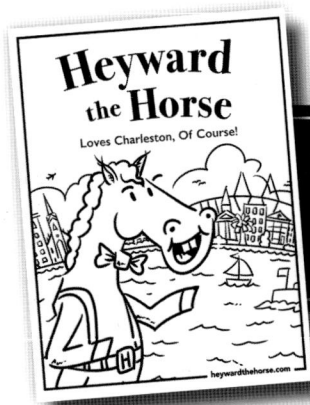

Looking for more Heyward fun?
Download FREE Heyward the Horse coloring sheets by visiting www.heywardthehorse.com/fun.